Animal
Bodies
UP
CLOSE

Nifty
NOSES
Up Close

Enslow Elementary
an imprint of
Enslow Publishers, Inc.
40 Industrial Road
Box 398
Berkeley Heights, NJ 07922
USA

http://www.enslow.com

Melissa
Stewart

CONTENTS

WORDS TO KNOW

blowholes (BLOH holhz)—The holes, or nostrils, on top of a whale's head. Whales breathe through the holes.

breathe (BREETH)—To take air in and let it out of the lungs.

nostrils (NAH struhlz)—The two openings of the nose.

oxygen (AHK suh jen)—A gas that has no color or smell. Living things need it to live.

tentacles (TEN tuh kuhlz)—Thin, flexible structures that some animals use to feel.

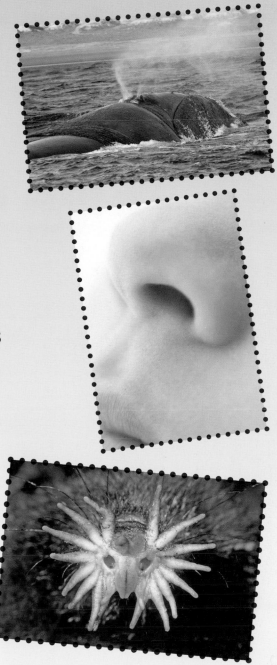

GIANT ANTEATER

Noses help animals in many ways. They smell and **breathe** and much, much more.

An anteater's nose can smell forty times better than your nose. It's perfect for tracking down ants and termites.

When an anteater chows down, it shuts its nose tight. That way insects can't crawl into its **nostrils**.

4

RIGHT WHALE

This whale has two nostrils on top of its head. They are called **blowholes**. They let the whale breathe without lifting its head out of the water.

POLAR BEAR

A polar bear has the best sense of smell on Earth. It uses its nose to hunt. It can sniff a dead seal from 20 miles (32 kilometers) away.

AFRICAN ELEPHANT

An elephant's trunk does more than just smell. It can grab food or rub an itchy eye. It can lift a branch or pick a flower. It can toot like a horn. And it can squirt water like a hose. What a nifty nose!

COHO SALMON

Each spring, these fish leave
the ocean. They swim into rivers
and streams. Then they mate and lay
eggs in the same place where they hatched.
How do the fish find just the right spot?
They sniff it out.

LEAF-NOSED BAT

This bat's nose helps it hunt flying insects. Its nose sends out high, squeaky sounds. When the sounds hit an insect, they bounce back. The echoes tell the bat where the insect is.

STAR-NOSED MOLE

Look at this mole's nose!

It has twenty-two pink **tentacles**.

As the mole digs through the ground,

its nose feels for worms and other food.

YOUR NOSE

You are an animal, too. Your nose takes air in—and lets it out—about seventeen thousand times a day. You use the **oxygen** in air to live, move, and grow.

Your nose tells you when cookies are baking. And it warns you when milk is sour.

GUESSING GAME

1. **A southern giant petrel (PEH truhl) uses its nose to . . .**

2. **An elephantnose fish uses its nose to . . .**

3. **A male proboscis (proh BOS kis) monkey uses its nose to . . .**

4. **A tapir (TAY per) uses its nose to . . .**

A. **grab plants and put them in its mouth.**

B. **find food buried in the seafloor.**

C. **get rid of the salt in the water it swallows.**

D. **attract mates.**

Write your answers on a piece of paper. Please do not write in this book!

See answers on page 24.

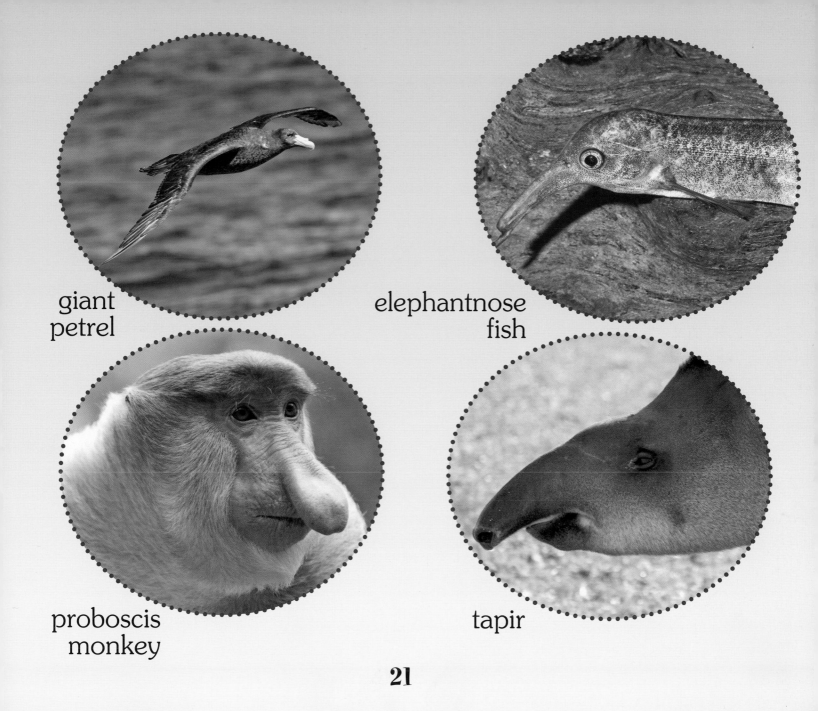

giant
petrel

elephantnose
fish

proboscis
monkey

tapir

LEARN MORE

Books

Hall, Peg. *Whose Nose Is This?* Mankato, Minn.:
Picture Window Books, 2007.

Jenkins, Steve, and Robin Page. *What Do You Do
with a Tail Like This?* Boston: Houghton Mifflin, 2008.

Miller, Sara Swan. *All Kinds of Noses.* Tarrytown, N.Y.:
Benchmark Books, 2007.

Randolph, Joanne. *Whose Nose Is This?* New York:
PowerKids Press, 2008.

Weiss, Ellen. *The Sense of Smell.* New York: Children's
Press, 2009.

WEB SITES

KidsHealth: Your Nose
<http://kidshealth.org/kid/
htbw/nose.html>

The NASA Sci Files:
The Sense of Smell
<http://scifiles.larc.nasa.gov/text/
kids/Problem_Board/problems/
stink/smell2b.html>

INDEX

Note to Parents and Teachers: The Animal Bodies Up Close series supports the National Science Education Standards for K–4 science. The Words to Know section introduces subject-specific vocabulary words, including pronunciation and definitions. Early readers may need help with these new words.

Enslow Elementary, an imprint of Enslow Publishers, Inc.

Enslow Elementary® is a registered trademark of Enslow Publishers, Inc.

Copyright © 2012 by Melissa Stewart

All rights reserved.

No part of this book may be reproduced by any means without the written permission of the publisher.

Library of Congress Cataloging-in-Publication Data
Stewart, Melissa.
   Nifty noses up close / Melissa Stewart.
      p. cm. — (Animal bodies up close)
   Includes bibliographical references and index.
   Summary: "Discover how different animals use their noses to smell and breathe and more"—Provided by publisher.
   ISBN 978-0-7660-3892-9 (alk. paper)
   1. Nose—Anatomy—Juvenile literature. I. Title.
   QL947.S638 2011
   599.14'4—dc22
                                        2011003339

Future editions:
Paperback ISBN 978-1-4644-0079-7
ePUB ISBN 978-1-4645-0986-5
PDF ISBN 978-1-4645-0986-2

Printed in China

012012 Leo Paper Group, Heshan City, Guangdong, China

10 9 8 7 6 5 4 3 2 1

To Our Readers: We have done our best to make sure all Internet Addresses in this book were active and appropriate when we went to press. However, the author and the publisher have no control over and assume no liability for the material available on those Internet sites or on other Web sites they may link to. Any comments or suggestions can be sent by e-mail to comments@enslow.com or to the address on the back cover.

Photo Credits: © 2011 Photos.com, a division of Getty Images, pp. 1, 3 (blowhole), 21 (proboscis monkey); © Alaska Stock / Alamy, p. 13; BananaStock/Thinkstock, p. 3 (nostrils); © Dwight Kuhn, pp. 3 (tentacles), 16; iStockphoto.com: © Adrian Assalve, pp. 2, 10, © David Parsons, p. 8, © kgfoto, p. 18, © Marshall Bruce (petrel), © Nina Shannon, p. 19; Minden Pictures: © Flip Nicklin, pp. 6, 7, © Tui De Roy, pp. 4, 5; Photo Researchers, Inc.: Dr. Merlin D. Tuttle/Bat Conservation International, p. 15, Mark Smith, p. 21 (elephantnose fish), Robert and Jean Pollock, p. 12, Rod Planck, p. 17, © SA Team, p. 14; Shutterstock.com, pp. 9, 11, 21 (tapir), 23.

Cover Photo: © 2011 Photos.com, a division of Getty Images

Series Literacy Consultant:
Allan A. De Fina, PhD
Dean, College of Education
Professor of Literacy Education
New Jersey City University
Past President of the New Jersey Reading
   Association

Science Consultant:
Helen Hess, PhD
Professor of Biology
College of the Atlantic
Bar Harbor, Maine

Answers to the Guessing Game
Southern giant petrel: C. get rid of the salt in the water it swallows.
Elephantnose fish: B. find food buried in the seafloor.
Male proboscis monkey: D. attract mates.
Tapir: A. grab plants and put them in its mouth.
